JOYCE WILLIAMS, a former
Grammar School, worked in
a printing firm until her marria

After her children were bor
LLCM and taught music and speech. Later she obtained an honours BA and BSc with the Open University. A prolific writer and poet, her short stories and poems were published in magazines for many years and broadcast on radio, notably her children's stories on *Listen with Mother.*

Joyce's first poetry collection, *Open Window*, was originally published in 2010 and republished by SilverWood Books in 2012.

Joyce was working on her autobiography when she died unexpectedly in February 2009 after a short illness.

WALKING THE DOG

JOYCE WILLIAMS

SilverWood

Published in 2018 by SilverWood Books

SilverWood Books Ltd
14 Small Street, Bristol, BS1 1DE, United Kingdom
www.silverwoodbooks.co.uk

Please read the poetic language used throughout this collection in relation to the context and era in which it was written.

ISBN 978-1-78132-764-7

British Library Cataloguing in Publication Data
A CIP catalogue record for this book is available from the British Library

Page design and typesetting by SilverWood Books
Printed on responsibly sourced paper

For Joyce, with much love,
David

Acknowledgements

Poetry is the essence of emotional experience
distilled in appropriate language.
Joyce Williams (2008)

With these words my wife set out what poetry meant to her, and I hope that the poems in this collection help as examples of this.

Following on from the success of her first collection, *Open Window*, and after requests to see more of her work, I have made this further collection of her poems.

My task was greatly aided by help from Pamela Marchant and David Johnson who read through the poems I sent them, picking out those that appealed to them most, and thereby making my selection of 80 poems less subjective. For this and for their kind advice and interest I offer my sincere thanks.

I would also like to thank Lois Aizlewood for the illustrations throughout the book. Her very close friendship with Joyce, going back to their childhood, is evidenced by her sympathetic pictures.

Last, but not least, thanks are due to Helen Hart and the SilverWood team for their patience and expertise.

David Williams

Contents

Time

Place

People

Nature

Time

...they hear in that heart the drum roll of centuries

Summer Was Measureless

Summer was measureless; each full-blown day
Turned timelessly about its axis – noon,
While lessons grew more humdrum with the croon
Of captive flies. What punishment to stay
Indoors when out-of-doors invited play –
The high wide sky (the sun a bluff buffoon)
The common, and the elm tree hollow-hewn,
The new made stack of prickly, tickly hay…
Measureless it was; we did not gauge
The fulsome splendour of its lighted stage,
Nor estimate its bounty flower by flower,
Nor strain the fragrance of a thunder shower,
But magnified each moment as it fell,
And lived a hundred summers in its spell.

Locked Out

The darkful garden drips with dismal rain.
Locked out I wait; no light shines near at hand.
The small gems quiver on the city's plain
And emphasise the dark, as here I stand
Where cats come pressing from the stealthy grass
With sodden fur. I wait; slow minutes pass.

The garden is a scribble of dark boughs
Against a pewter sky; and breathing, slack,
Amorphous bulk of restive yew, that soughs
With sound of shingle-rushing waves. The black
And empty shadows slither from my torch
And sidle up behind me in the porch.

Impregnable the house; bleak and aloof,
It offers no companionship. I lean,
Porch-sheltered, on the door, a heavy roof
Drum-throbbing overhead. And now a keen
Wind desperately that tugs the straining gate
Throws sharp rain in my face. I lean and wait.

Sandcastle Fancies

Dancing on the morning shore,
World turned to greet the tide of days,
In summer haze
We flung sandcastle fancies forth.
The waters met them,
Cradled and set them rocking, rocking, rocking.

Racing down the corridor,
Wide windows opening on a high
Embattled sky,
We gave our noisy notions birth
Echoes multiplied them
As sea birds came and cried them, flocking,
flocking, flocking.

Looking for the open door
In streets of strangers winding, long,
Without a song
We gather up our fancies' worth –
Sun in the westward sky,
Sound of the seagulls' cry mocking, mocking, mocking.

Windows

Many windows turn towards the west
Red-lidded on the hill; a monochrome
Of crimson indiscriminately flung
At evening blinds their futile hopes and woes,
Smudging them all to silence. And they drowse
Until the sun, engaging in its slot,
Draws darkness down, and then they stir and blink
And wake and come to life and show themselves –
Boldly exhibiting, coy or secretive –
Their little lives imperfectly enacted,
Square or oblong-bound, flicked on or off
By switch or curtain, snapshots disconnected,
Fragments of a drama randomly performed.

At last they peter out and sleep again
Until the shifting minutes bring the light.
Then many windows turning to the west
Show black or shining as the day decides,
Revealing nothing in the working hours,
Saving their ritual performances –
Unfinished tragedies and comedies –
Their pantomimes and human mysteries –
For curtain-up on yet another night.

Fossils

These stones turned up by plough and garden spade –
(Shapely shell-shapes, coils and whorls,
Some steeply embossed as to suggest
The imprint of mechanical presses,
Others like pale and early snapshots
Mere whispers of themselves) –
Are hunted through the limestone quarries
By students and geologists with hammers
For once these stones had life! – and lived! –
Their home the shifting waters
That gnawed this peak of oolite, this belvedere,
This village famed for fossils and its view;
And here they are – impossibly perpetual,
Yet they are here. And we who are not scientists
May also make
Collection and selection for fireplace and boundary wall,
And feel a kind of awe
And the sentiment we feel
For household pets deceased,
As if the live stones could have recognised
And come to the call of their sounding names:
Ammonite! Belemnite! Sediments of an age
Of massive simplicity and slow-hauling time,
A time for growing old. Can these stones speak –
Declare things aren't the same since man took over?
Fossils diminish one, but they have a way
Of putting things in perspective.

Women in Kaleidoscope

You in the morning – morning of your day –
You – two years old – had found your mother's shoes
And staggered round already one of us,
Preened in the long glass, laughed and clopped away,
Woman all through.
Now on this summer bridge it's afternoon – but morning still for you –
And leaning from the stronghold of a father's arms
You crow at your reflection
Creased and dimpling in the shallows, and I see
A hundred women's glances in that upturned face.

You are your mother's mothers many ages back;
I see their private anguish as they wave men off to war,
I see them laugh and weep and suffer
With the ones they love
As ripples bend and break,
A continuous kaleidoscope
World over through all time
While you a baby journey from a morning's joy
To present day. I see a small coquette
Become a schoolgirl then a graduate and then –
What then – career or motherhood? Or both?
And will each age outjoy the one before
Or ripples break in sorrow and regret?
This is the conundrum of our state, and how we meet
The hurrying current of the age –
Pliant as river weed or else as pebbles
Stalwart yet smoothed by many waters' flow –
We re-determine day by passing day.

And you will strive to influence the river's course,
Direct its passage. Sometimes you'll succeed.
But always you'll be one with us – at two
Or twenty two or twice again.
We are more free
Than we have ever been yet we remain
Linked to each other as the ripples break
And gather through all time throughout the turning world.

Pandora

I couldn't stop him even if I tried –
He wed the fatal box when he wed me.
"Go on," I tell him. "What will be will be –
"Curiosity must be satisfied.
"Unclasp and lift the lid, and peer inside,
"Probe the cosmos, split the nucleus – free
"Mankind from ignorance – we need to see
"Whether the virtual cat has lived or died!"

The rest is history, as the saying goes.
Out they all swarmed like bloated blowflies – black,
Vile and putrid – plagues, famines, warfare, woes…
We beat them off but couldn't put them back.
"But that's not all" – he cried – "the box contains".
"For look – the last one's Hope!" And Hope remains.

Eclipse

The inexorable moon
slow-wheels its ordered track,
advancing on our sun
until a black
disc of darkness
overtakes the source
of intellectual power,
encompassing its splendour,
counterchanging light
with negativity
until
a cold stillness,
silent, stark
as Arctic winter falls
upon our helplessness.

Daylight extinguished
we feel a chill
of deathly emptiness,
before breathtakingly we see
that, body devoured,
the soul remains
–corona in glory–
and we have been
vouchsafed a sight
of what has always been,
and whether the darkness moves
or stays
is there and will remain.

A Village Eve

This is Nellie – raucous at sundown now
Proud-bellied, huge athwart the track
That calls itself a highway through this hamlet
Hauling her fish-eyed progeny from play.
Surely you know her – see the spade-hard hands,
The straddled stance; clammy the hair that falls
Like sea-brown weed on boulders,
Massive the swelling shoulders – Nellie is everywhere.

For this is she who wept
At Waterloo – who cried
At Crecy – and whose groans
Were heard at Hastings when the Conqueror killed.
See her – the mother – (you know her now) –
Cursing and kissing,
Cuffing, caressing ...they hear in that heart
The drum roll of centuries,
And earth that turns in turmoil also clings
To her steadfast feet. She will not brush it away.

The Visionary

What is his vision, enigmatic fish
Emerging copper-scaled as waters
Shrink back dark like treacle
Under red, volcanic skies?
On his fins will he prophesy this
Father of amphibians?

For this is Evolution – does he see
His progeny reptile-begotten
Some claw-toed, dagger-toothed,
Some heavy like warships
Tied up in times of peace, wallowing
Among the flaccid sallows of moist, slow,
Swollen, thunder-footed days –
Days of creation?

Will he foresee, this pioneering fish
The grotesque lizard-shapes
Lumbering cumbrous through swamp
And steaming vegetation?
And those unregarded creature-lings –
The runted progeny –
Trampled underfoot, warm, furred
And insignificant?

What does he dream – supposing that he dreams
This far-off day of molten sun –
Is it that to the brainchild of that small, warm brood
A million ages hence Creation will submit –
His to continue
Or destroy?

Heroes

In the beginning of the age
I watched my Heroes,
brown-bearded, head-high,
riding from Asgard –
their blue eyes ice sharp,
alight with songs and laughter –
sounds of their horses' hooves
like hammering of artillery
against the sky,
as they went fearlessly out in laughter and song
to do battle with wicked deeds
of gods and men.

At the end of the age
I see them return,
frost-bearded, head-hung, sombre-eyed,
singing no song –
victors yet not victorious,
for they have learned
that the wolf has grown strong
in their absence,
and the slow serpent heaves in the darkness of many
oceans.
They are no longer young, my Heroes;
the enemy is here in our midst –
there is battle still to do,
and they sing no song.

Innocence

To be innocent
Is to be unaware:
Here on the spread grass
Meeting the cathedral's front
A child marvels at daisies,
Tenderly probing each ochre eye
With a questioning finger,
And we recognise something lost.

Within the prayer-filled space
Limestone enfolded
A still candle
Reassures,
Its steadfast flame
Shredded, torn apart
Like daisy petals -
He loves me – he loves me not – he loves me –
In turmoil of un-creation.
Yet here
(We venture to believe)
is holy simplicity,
And the flame snuffed out
Trails fragments of fragrant smoke
Like incense –
A kind of innocence.

Musica Reservata

Here is no sterile perfection of mealy-mouthed
Instruments in well-mannered melody;
A country dialect this, untutored,
Ringed with bright overtones like children's chatter,
Like chattering children too outspoken
For acceptable behaviour in an adult world.
Why then the thrill to this ancient music
And the pull of an old nostalgia
Down deep in the heart of things?

For here is no perfection – we can hear
Those crude mechanics of their sound,
And the raw, uncompromising notes
Fall on the ear with a sort of shout
Astonishing the senses.
Then why this longing and the appetite unfed
Though we wax fat on refinement, sniff
The scentless bloom, praise featureless creatures
In accents factory-fresh and free from dross?
How can we know the craving of that child within
For a wilder, sweeter fruit
As the white bread turns to ashes on the tongue?

Barabbas

Libation poured waits casting away of the vessel
And this I know; that wine
Without a vessel cannot be contained
Nor a libation poured. Uncomprehendingly
I gaze into the depth of me;
I am the vessel – base metal only,
Yet went from me a richness and a potency
That I grew drunk on, and I'll never know
What fashioned me to do this service.
Service I say? Freedom or service, they are the same
I only know that this was done and work was wrought
Through me, and through me brought to consummation.
I pass from history – a vessel only, turned in relentless fingers,
Yet with a halting certainty that cast away,
My own gross surface will reflect
The splendour of that Light, and I shall see.

Easter

Easter comes in every season – not only
In the youth-time of year
When day's eye opens
On a wash of green and gold,
And threads of song
Begin to be heard
With first stirrings
In hedge and thicket;
But whenever – wherever –
A shared smile flickers
Between strangers in a lonely place;
Unfolding buds of hope
Lift glimmering heads
In a detritus of worn-out ends,
And the human heart
Dreading a dark door
Discovers it already ajar, and light within;
There is a beginning – a birth –
A burst of joy –
And Easter comes.

Before the (Written) Exam

TUTOR: I'm confident you'll all do well!
If you have ears to hear
the written notes inside your head
you've nothing much to fear.

Be sure when writing in four parts
to check out every bar;
you need to show the examiner
all you have learnt so far.

When harmonising melodies
e.g. – for voice or flute –
NEVER double the leading note.
(It's safe to double the root.)

Avoid consecutives – octaves, fifths.
If you let the leading note fall
you should ask yourself if you're fit to be
on this course at all.

(Yes, Bach can get away with it
and Handel breaks the rules,
but genius can please itself,
the rules were made for fools.)

...continue in free piano style
an opening melody...?
(You'll be required to modulate
so bear in mind the key.)

...realise a figured bass...?
Write out a turn and shake...?
Mean-tone...? Tritone...? Keep your cool –
it's all a piece of cake!

STUDENT: So – nothing to fear from this exam
theoretical and tactical?
There's just one thing I'm dreading more
– and that's the practical!

Two Minutes

Bare branches criss-crossed like bayonets against blue sky
Crisp cold air
Marching feet
Banners tugged by the brisk wind
Brownies and Sea Scouts (do they understand),
Choir in a line outside the church near war memorial.
Village cat takes up position.
Wreaths are laid, lines spoken
Trumpet falters
Lips numbed by cold and nervousness.
Rumbling tractor lumbering by.
Dogs bark from garden of village pub
then fall silent.
All fall silent.
So many minutes here in the churchyard.
So many minutes gathered together.
So many minutes across countries
Minutes – moments – swelling globes.
All hopes, fears, thoughts, prayers, remembrances,
bewilderment – what thoughts do the children
think in these two, lengthening minutes.
Two minutes lives-worth given for so many
years of given lives.

(*Impossible not to think in terms of war this day*)

The Secret

Like a balloon it swells and tugs its string.
Let it go free? My sandals in the dust
stir patterns. Idling on my garden swing,
the doubtful schoolday done, I yield and trust
my secret to the next-door cat. Now – rust
and rose – brick walls enclose a memory:
the clothes-line swing, the tree, the silver crust
of apple-bloom, a cobalt sky… I see,
stretched out, a striped cat blinking sunlight back at me.

Sun – and a secret shared – and solitude –
each day a rising goblet filled with light –
a boundary with no edge – from which I viewed
as through a lens my own small childhood –
tight-buttoned, closeted from all that might
come near. Home is the world, the swing my space,
the apple tree a fortress. All is bright
with promise. Satisfied, seduced, I trace
the patterned dust with feet secure in their own place.

When did the sun go in, the blossom fall?
My swing, dismantled, leaves the garden bare.
The cat streaks back across the garden wall,
there is a threat of thunder in the air.
This secret weighs too heavily to share:
shut doors distort the taunts, the whispering,
the threatened tit-for-tat. So – show I care?
They'd only say, 'It isn't anything.'
But then – why did he take her clothes-line for my swing?

Time in a Nutshell

How shall it be defined?
We capture it with clocks
Only to have it slip
Mercury-like in broken beads
From confines of hours and centuries,
Seasons turning to decay,
And childhood yesterdays that seem
Nearer than today.

Yet common sense recoils
From the notion that we are not bound
To a single rail
Travelling all one way.
We cannot quite accept
That rods contract,
That moving timepieces run slow
(Though, staring into space, we think we know
We see it as it used to be
Millennia ago.)

But how to describe
That moment poised
On the brink of Infinity,
Motion suspended and a sense
Of all things understood,
When we became aware
Of Space and Time
As one continuum,
Curved, borderless
And indivisible?

Einstein rode imagination
On a point of light.
Equations unravelling
From his office stool
Confirmed what Julien saw within her cell,
The small brown unregarded entity
That nestled in the palm of God:
'It is all that ever was and is
And All Manner Of Thing Shall Be Well.'

Place

This cottage as it used to look…sunk in it's rumpled bed

French Weir, Taunton, Somerset

Standing where I used to stand
Here on the walkway with the falls in spate
I see the river seem to hesitate
In slow brown flow,
Change its mind, divide,
And pour in languid motion
Over combed weed at the weir's edge
Before the swift, precipitate,
And unremitting slide
Below me and beneath as here I stand.

As here I stood –
How many, many times – a child
Compelled by voices giving tongue
In the descending water,
Controlled by its grand cacophony,
(A swelling globe encompassing those thoughts
That pounded at my ears
Imploring deliverance
Yet lacking words
To give them utterance and flight.)

My gaze was a grappling iron
To seize and stay
The plunge of one mere drop
In its appointed passage
Through those glittering skeins,
And watch it ride
Suspended in time and movement,
Its energy matched against my own,
Until I felt both eyes and brain would burst.
Then I, the weaker, overcome, would yield,

And turning, run to watch
The ferment on the walkway's other side,
Straining to catch
In the full-mouthed many-throated uproar
An individual message, small, particulate,
Fearing it impossible,
Fearing too that my encapsulated thoughts
With my whole self were being drawn and drowned,
Fragmented, pulverised and ground
To puffs of vapour on the rising spray…

Now standing as I used to stand
Here on the walkway with the falls in spate
I strive again to stay the drop of Time,
Wrest from its long descent
That other self who stood
Gazing and thinking on this selfsame spot.
What were the thoughts I struggled to express?
I only know I was a pilgrim to these falls;
Their power drew me then
And still enthralls.

Berkeley Square Garden

To be alive in Bristol
On a mid-May morning
Great George disgorging the hour
Into this pleasant garden hung
With roses plush pink,
Wisteria and bulbing knobs of figs,
Pots of pansies, wallflowers and
Pelargoniums caught in the act
Of clambering from their tubs and boxes.
Flag Irises thrusting gold tipped among Marsh Marigolds
And tumbling creeper and other mysteries
I cannot name cascading the steps.
To be here, cocooned and sheltered by old brick walls
And the city – my own city –
Enfolding me with its warm caress,
Is to be alive indeed.
A herring gull perches on a rail
And fixes me with fishy eye.
A crane, skeletal and shapely, rises beyond the buildings
And ducks swoop across my blue and white of sky.
I am in the midst of industry
Yet here there is tranquility.
A breeze fingers the growing things,
Shuffles the shadows in the sycamore
That reaches down from a high wall,
Its roots somewhere above my head.
I have retreated into this womb of quietness
Within a city.

Entropy

Weston-super-Mare – the tide far out,
A silver line beyond the glistening ooze.
The grown ups said the ozone did them good.
At school I learned that what they sniffed
And relished was the smell –
Ozone was something else.

Oh in those donkey riding,
Ice cream licking days I knew a lot –
The atmosphere for instance
Is a mixture, mostly nitrogen.
(What if its mere one fifth of oxygen
Should gather itself together and recede
With Weston's tide,
Leaving us to drown like fish in empty air?)

'Entropy,' the teacher said. 'Disorder rules.
Once mixed, things never of themselves unmix.
The life-sustaining entity will always be
Present in the air we breathe.'

Comforting thought. Yet here and now we two,
With schooldays farther off than Weston's tide
Released at lunchtime from a meeting held
At Weston-super-Mare,
Have left our colleagues mixing in the bar
With those who cannot of themselves unmix,
And take our sandwiches and walk out on the pier
Over the mud, and breathe the smell
(Or should we call it ozone?)
And congratulate ourselves –
Two migrant molecules and free as air,
Exceptions setting out to prove the rules.

Winter Fire

Today
In curiosity
I join the wishful-thinkers
Looking round
A new apartment
In a much-to-be-desired
Locality,
Said to be
The very latest word
In luxury.

We tread
The under-heated floors,
Admire kitchen gadgetry
And bathroom wizardry,
Astonishing wide-angle views –
But gazing
Through triple glazing
At traffic slinking
Silently
I dream myself
A different luxury:

Crackling of coal and spurt of flame,
Shadows and firelight fingering patterns
On shifting walls
Of rose and orange and grey –
Texture of hearthside rug
Scrunched between my toes –
Fragrance of fire-warmed winceyette
And a high white bed
Waiting and wide –
Sound of rain on the glassy black
Of an ill-fit sash,
A stormy moon beyond
Bowled by rolling clouds –
Companionable sounds of trains and calling owls,
Slow tick of the downstairs clock,
Ripple of voices from the kitchen below –
Fireglow filling my room with friendship,
Sensuousness, luxury.

Hospital Ward

Down the white passages of pain
They glide in a dream,
Borne by intensity of lifetime
Pressed to a measured span.
Days revolve in slow sterility
Recorded days of drugs and charts
Cool voices urging confidence –
The antiseptic days
And unreality
Of morning papers and the meal time humour
Visitors tongue-tied or wearisome –
Vacuum between realities
Of life and death.
Nights stalk in a soft soled silence
Through whispered pulse of headphones disregarded
And spasmodic jerk of the clock
While petals slip untallied in a corridor
Among the labelled jars.

Candles in a Church

Here are candles in a holy place:
Here innocence and purity
Offer a homily
To the simple-hearted,
Their calm intensity
Shedding lustre on wooden
Lectern, pew and pulpit,
Evoking remembered prayer
And peace beyond all understanding.

But look –
Is not this steady radiance
The perpetual outpouring
Of a self-sustaining light?
Could we but apprehend
In its soft effulgence
The maelstrom within each flame,
The energy,
The sundering of selfsame molecules
That make the stuff of what we are,
And see our seething fabric – incandescent –
Primitive particles destroyed and mended
In a storm of plasma –
Then might we comprehend the power
That brought to being all creation
And upholds its laws,
And say with sage and prophet: 'God is light!'

* * *

Candles in a holy place
Burning with quiet intensity
Tell of the mystery
At the heart of things.

The Question Mark

Remember it? This cottage as it used to look?
Almost too paintbox-pretty, sunk in its rumpled bed,
Those bee-heavy blooms
Tumbling over the roadside wall,
And that smug dog,
Colour of barley sugar in the sun,
Sqatting before the gate, tongue fluttering,
Adoring summer,
Snug in his idle days?

So long ago when love took leave;
Summer and sunshine, garden and golden dog – all gone,
An angry son the last to stride away
From that cottage in its wintertime
Which crouches now, gaping to metal sky
And a thin moon
That tingles like a question mark,
High over the vanished blooms
Sunk under snow bruised by departing feet.

When did the bitterness begin
That caused decay? And had it never been,
Could we imagine life again inside these walls,
Lights at the windows,
Warmth in the chimney,
Berries around the door,
And another dog fluttering a snow-specked tongue,
Adoring all seasons,
Snug in the glow of love?

Sonnet at Stanton Drew

Older, older than the tales told
Of wedding party turned to stone
That danced across the midnight bound
Into a forbidden Sabbath;
Older, older than the prosings
Of bone dry archeologists,
The fantasisings
Of astrologists, ufologists and sociologists;
Older, older than the physicist's
Fractured second
Is the power-imparting Power
That breathed upon these standing stones
Aeons before they lurched
In a gathered circle
Tingling with force
Beyond all understanding,
Frozen energy

Kept in thrall
By the selfsame Power
That holds the nucleus
Within the atom
Within each fragment
Within each stone.
Myths, legends, theories and hypotheses –
These
Are no more than humdrum
Guesses at a conumdrum, a mystery
Older, older than the singularity
Beyond which all things cease to be
And we are turned to stone – amazed –
Like wedding guests who danced
On, on into a Sabbath day
That has no ending.

Ghosts

The ghost of what you were a moment past
Lingers in your smile.
I try to grasp the essence of that Present and bring it into
Now.
But Now dissolves in past and future;
I cannot conjugate the verb – there are only
The idea and the infinitive.
Echoes of what has been and what will be
Mingle in one music, a threnody that spins
And binds us in a single chord,
So that we seem the ghosts of what's to come
Who gaze through a diminishing lens
At what we were, and what we might have been.
Here, as you smile, I watch the trees
Shuffle their summer leaves in sunlight,
Spattering patterns of shade
On this path that leads to the fieldgate,
A sudden barrier set square in space. Beyond –
Warm tilt of grassgrown slope

(Colour of cats' eyes in the August heat)
Gleams indolent, empty of all save ghosts.
Once, in another Now, a child and her father
Crossed its face through autumn dampness to go nutting
In those high woods that mark its bounds,
Diffusing sky-enamelled blue to chalk-grey dustiness.
The voices, journeying, journeyed, journey on through time;
I catch the cadences but inwardly – their substance
Cannot cross the fieldgate.
The sun burns brighter, and the shades of what they were
Stir in the shifting leaves. What do the trees know?
That we are restless ghosts
For ever seeking Now in past and future,
Translucent as these sliding leaves above our heads?
We cannot linger in this Present – its echoes
Vibrate in time and travel into space
Whilst the ghost of what you were a moment past
(A nanosecond or a thousand million years? – the same)
Lingers in your smile.

Remembered City

The sloping meadows reach and grasp the fringe
Of sprawling city. Here on this high hill
I watch advancing summer warmly tinge
The distant living thing. How strangely still,
Vulnerable beneath the open sky,
The silent city lies and makes no sound.
How strangely past, that silent time when I
Was daily part of all its daily round.
Aloof I gaze and sort the jumbled view.
Where do the well-remembered buildings stand?
The newsprint columns of the starkly-new
Obscure the old, and rise on every hand.
I turn away. Around me here is all
Young summer, green and full of cuckoo's call.

Two Rivers

Two rivers flowed,
Three bridges crossed the Avon;
One of the three – or sometimes all – I took each working day:
Redcliffe – the bascule bridge that rose on end
Letting commerce in or out,
Or Ha'penny Bridge beyond the cradling bend
That crawled by the walls of George's brewery,
Or Bristol Bridge that gave the town its name;
And under each the Avon khaki-grey
Lapped a slippery passageway to meet
The wider waters of the Severn sea.

Two rivers –
One bore traffic on its back
For Godwin Warren and the Sand & Gravel Co. They've gone
But Harry Brown still scuttles with the tide;
The ferries and the pleasure craft
Now furrow a cleaner surface, scattering swans
Of paler whiteness than they were before
That gather for bounty
At the floating restaurant's side;
Times change and rivers flow.

And rivers flow –
What of that other effluence, the Frome
Gliding through dripping walls beneath the beat
Of busy feet above?
We ride the highway, tread the street, ignore
That groping thing.
Cold, black and silent, breathing in its tomb
It slinks and slithers as those visions slide
That trouble dreams, half grasped, half understood,
And sometimes bubble up and overwhelm
The consciousness of day-to-day.

Two rivers flow,
The one above, the other out of sight and out of mind.
One moves and changes with the changing times,
The other, channelled and confined,
Bides well its time.

The Way to the Sea

Here foxgloves thrust magenta satin bells
Through tangled brambles and proud living gold
Of varied blossoms. Honey-sweet are smells
About the hedgerow, mingling with the bold
Rough salty tang of wetted rock and surf.
But look beyond the roses: see – between
Tall ivied sycamores, the curving turf
Is peachbloom-cropped on layered cliffs that lean
Their balding foreheads into smoking spray.
Now climb the gate, and leave the lane to wind
Through shaggy banks. The wide serrated bay
Claims silence and all sounds; time's left behind,
And here the moving tide is big with sea,
Whose potent emptiness swells endlessly.

The Field

In the field autumn stained
The lurching monoliths observe
A ritual with the sky.
The child goes shouting through the wet grass
Scattering cattle
Shattering atmosphere in ecstasy.
The rain grained massive stones are his
Unhallowed now to climb, explore
And to abandon for the chestnut's bounty
Vermillion on milky linings of suede;
And the staid field quickens exulting
In present wonder.
But laughter and child depart; the living dead
Close in communion as the sky comes down
And seem to ruminate
The slow imponderable everlasting turn of time.

Cliff Climb

Now reeling sky shakes in kaleidoscope
Breakers and broken cries of gulls outflung
Upon conflicting winds, and small and brown
The butterflies that tantalize his strength.
Ears ring with blood; there was an easier way –
A tamed path winding upward from the cove –
But being boy he chose the climb and hangs
Lonely against a sky swinging its arc
Over and under with the lunging sea.
A moment motionless, clamped to the face
That stretches endlessly, – above, – below…
Then nerve returns – he flings him on the height,
Breathless, and hears throughout the timeless pause
Drowned sound of surf in steadfast long applause.

Heritage

Redly the new house gapes on the hill
Like a raw wound,
And frustrated wind shouting at corners
Blinds with a smarting flak.
Birds and raped woods crouch sullenly
Waiting encroachment
Of years to give decent burial.
But surely age will never soothe and mollify
That angry indignity…

Then – with a slow spade turning clods –
They found the coin,
Rubbed and irregular with passage of palms
For generations dust.
At once the house, taking form,
Grafted and grew to the sweet earth,
A live thing drawing breath
In the programme and pulse of time.

Cross-Boising in the Channel

Fragment of a dream

It was a picture that erupted into view
Seconds ahead of waking, and I knew
Its title had been there for ever –
'Cross-boising in the Channel' –
Branded on the frame that grew and grew
Until it overwhelmed my seeing eye,
And all at once I understood the whole
Of everything, its when and why.
        But now – what were they, those fantastic slim ship-shapes
        With lithe translucent hulls of black and gold,
        And gauzy sails
        Iridescent like the wings of damsel flies?
        Unhelmed they sported of their own accord,
        And coursed and hunted, dodged and doubled,
        Patterning a sea jewel-tinted, scintillating
        With an aching brilliance.
        I asked: "What is it that they do?
        What meaning in their message?"
        The graven words themselves replied:
        "*Cross-boising in the Channel.*"
Then momently I knew and could express
Their pure and unselfconscious joy,
But morning broke into my dream, its light
Revealed an empty screen, the picture fled.
And yet I know that somewhere near at hand
Though out of sight
They are cross-boising in the channel still,
And there is meaning in their motion,
And it is true…
And beautiful…
And right.

This Window

This window is the one that draws me most
Not for its view but for its drapery
Of ivy scrambling over frame and sill,
Smothering stark Euclidean lines
In random distribution
Of thin-veined angled hearts
That range from saucer size to some
No larger than a baby's finger nail.

Translucent slender sinews travel up the pane
Combing the glass with ranks of tender feet
Like elongated millipedes
That bear the green new growth upon their backs.

And nestling in the folds are bulls-eye whirls

Of snails that quest with quivering horns
On slim transparent necks, and cobwebs
Glittering in an after-shower sun.

I shall be sorry when we cut it down –
A private grief – but it will grow again.
It has the calm, unhurried air
Of one that knows his worth and doesn't care.

Chance Meeting in the Check-Out Queue

Chance meeting in the check-out queue –
Her eyes appraise his eyes of blue,
She likes his smile and cuddly frame,
She'd rather like to ask his name
(How would it seem if she inquired –
A business woman, just retired?)
'I'm Christabel,' she volunteers,
And he replies, 'My name is Piers,
A doting grandfather of four,
And widower ten years or more.'

Now moving slowly with the queue,
Exchanging chat and points of view
On art, philosophy and such,
They're pleased to find that they have much
In common, that they fondly share
A taste for Proust and Baudelaire,
And that they steadfastly avoid
The works of Jung and Sigmund Freud.
Oh, happy chance that brings these two
Together in the check-out queue!

Oh, happy chance, that heart-to-heart
Reveals their bent in books and art,
And is the very same for each!
And when eventually they reach
The check-out counter it's as though
They were 'an item' years ago
Instead of just ten minutes since
Between the marmalade and mince!
And each dares wonder: 'Could this be
A meeting that was meant for me?'

Now from her trolley, low-fat spread
And veggie meals and slimmers' bread
Appear to his astonished gaze;
He thinks (while noting in a daze
Those Health Care pills for this and that)
'She'll be allergic to my cat!'
While Christabel sees, close to tears,
The guilty trolley hauled by Piers –
Cans of cat food, tins of ham,
Butter, pickles, cheeses, jam…

They pay in silence, leave the store,
Then face each other just once more.
'Goodbye. It's been nice meeting you,
And chatting in the check-out queue.'
Home she'll go to sterile flat
While Piers finds comfort with his cat;
They feel a tugging at the heart,
A little sadness as they part,
But loading up each empty car,
Both think they're best off as they are.

People

At the ritual gate they'll linger an hour maybe in mute scrutiny of meadow

Sonnet on a Bonnet

Here is her bonnet! How like her to throw
The finished thing aside, and hatless run
To meet high summer in her own glad glow,
Leaving behind this token of the sun –
This hat she trimmed for something fresh to do,
With pouting poppies, sultry and intense;
With cornflowers, blue as her own eyes are blue,
And happy daisies, white as innocence.
She's gone – but left her very self behind;
This hat proclaims her – careless, bright and bold,
Yet tender as these flowers you see entwined,
Sweet as summer, young as Time is old.
She is not here – but this discarded bonnet
Still bears her testimonial upon it.

The Artist

Down in the village
An old Welshman
Has been painting a gate
This summer-long afternoon
Lovingly laying the colour on as if he were
Some Celtic Constable, and the gate his canvas.
The plot behind is up for sale,
Shortly to be submerged, no doubt, beneath
Bungaloid overgrowth, white-paled perhaps
Or trapped in tortuous topiary – the gate will be redundant.
But he lays the colour on
Stroke by meticulous stroke, absorbed in creation,
While those tall grasses wave under the elder bloom
And loaf-sugar cottages glisten amid geraniums
Against a backcloth of Wedgwood loud with larks.
An artist, he knows
How best to waste the idle afternoon,
And does it to perfection.

Winter

The fire is out;
No winter log
Fuelled by summer's flame
Gives breath to chimneys sighing out
Longings of childhood.
Not now.
And anyway the charge no doubt
Today would be
Unlawful entry, for
The heart and hearth are empty, and
The fire is out.

The fire is out –
They may not scramble on my knee,
Play with my beard
Or whisper in my ear.
I'm not allowed to hug or touch.
Depriving and deprived
I hand the parcels out,
And when at last the sack sags empty
Hear them say
(Hear with dismay):
"Those whiskers aren't for real –
You're just a bloke dressed up."
I go away
Back to the ashen hearth.
The party's over, and
The fire is out.

Reconciliation

A rabbit, would you say,
This one-eared bitten thing,
Grey with grime
Of half a century at least,
Limp-limbed and shedding sawdust
On the path?

The single button-eye looks up
In desperate appeal:
"Finish me; burn me;
I have outlived my life
And now, replaced, am flung
Useless, unloved aside."

But wait – a little trotting boy
With busy steps comes scolding
Down the lane,
Chides in his mother's voice,
Chastens with hurtless hand
The errant straggler left behind;
Then gathers into cherishing arms,
Forgives it, and stumbles away.

A Journey in Fog

Fog is an aberation. Fog opaque,
And flocculent, heavy like felted wool
Cocoons this bus-encapsulated load, who rub
The wall-eyed windows only to behold
Their shuddering reflections mop and mow.
Fog is a kind of madness, binding mind
As well as eyes, and sense as well as mind.
Where are we now? The bus pulsates and grinds;
I feel it sliding – sliding back and back,
backwards and sideways to the river – no!
Let me get out! I panic through the press
Then in the blank outside, I realize
The vehicle is stationary. Fool!
Faces loom and vanish – some perplexed,
Others amused, incredulous. I think
That this is what it must be to be old –
The reason swathed and suffocated, fogged,
Enfolded, and the body sliding back,
Backwards and sideways, back towards the river.

Lights at Night

I have a memory of lights at night –
The homeward hillside trudge, myself at three
Complaining, tired, not tall enough to see.
They lifted me and set at shoulder height:
"Just look my darling – such a pretty sight! –
Why – now it's vanished!" (Stooping, teasing me.)
"Look, there they are again!" And there would be
The twinkling town spread out for my delight.
For my delight? I wrenched my head aside,
Sought comfort in a grown-up shoulder, cried,
But could not tell them what distressed me so:
How that I'd seen a hopelessness below,
(The pathos of it all!) Each light a spark
Futile against the overwhelming dark.

Cousins Meet

Cityscape beyond the slatted blinds;
Red cloth, the pale wine shimmering,
Cool on the lips and dry.

Murmurs advance, recede like waves on shingle,
Fragrances mingle in skeins of warmth
As dishes are brought.

Savour the wine, the food, the atmosphere,
Consanguinity continuing as we meet
And eat, remembering when.

Faces

Light gets in the way of looking.
I long to see around the corner of a smile,
What lies behind an eyelid, sits within a skull.
But light gets in the way.

I see the faces sharp in sunlight,
Soft in shadow, haunting in candleglow;
The moving lightplay glints
On changing glances, getting in the way.

Come over to the window; let me look.
Take off the masks and make-up.
But even as you do the light shines in my eyes
Too brightly and gets in the way.

A Woman Waiting

Every morning
On the station platform
Waiting the arrival of the early train
She slops around
In too-big shoes, frowns at the toy
Wristwatch on her skinny arm, and seems
Impatient, important;
        She mustn't be kept
            Waiting.

The train comes in –
        Handshakes and hugs,
            Hurryings, harrowings,
                Partings, dispersal,
                    Sucking in, spitting out,
                        Moving on, rejecting,
                            Leaving her

Slopping around in too-big shoes
Comparing her watch with the station clock,
Waiting the arrival of another train,
Living out her fantasy
    Of living
      A life.

What happens when
The last train leaves,
The red eye of its tail light
Blinking in the blackness
Of the tunnel,
    Of the night, of the womb, of the grave?
      Do they let her wait
        In the waiting room
          Waiting
            For morning, waiting
              For life, waiting
                For death,
                  Waiting?

Black Girl

Here, where symbolic scars that weave and whirl
(Signature of some exotic race)
Are blemishes upon an alien face,
She unbelonging stands – a coloured girl.
Willing prisoner of a self-made cage,
Remoulded now, to foreign speech and thought,
Learning forgetfulness of what was taught
Her in a far-off land, a distant age.
And yet she unbelonging stands, for she,
Wanderer to a new world from the old,
Indelibly committed, may not hold
To either, yet they will not set her free.
Her children's children will belong and own
A heritage. But now she stands alone.

The Bookseller

In the doorway of his shop coffin-shaped
That spilled its lore on to the pavement
He would stand holding an open book,
And you went in and out like a burrowing worm
Through a hoard of homeless leaves
And pathos of faded messages between damp boards;
Never a word from him as he turned his page,
But through the twin bowls of his spectacles
The light eyes swam like little fish
Leaping for learning in a pool of printed words.

Portrait

The man who talks with trees
Has gone up the snow-frosted hill,
A lean dog loping alongside.
He knows more of the lore of nature and her ways
Than you learn in a lifetime; but little he says,
And you would not fret sublime simplicity
With trivialities.

Soon at the ritual gate they'll linger
Man and dog an hour maybe
In mute scrutiny of meadow, wood and moving skies.
He breathes the sunlight, and his sensitive finger feels
A quickening of small pulses through the cold.
Meet him along the byway and he'll bid
A shy good day, and you may read
An almanac in his changing eyes.

A Song for JDB

I saw you in the wan rain
Of that day's premature fall
Wrapped in a pewter sheen
Of sky and hueless city shapes –
A day for lamenting
And you were singing.

Yours were ephemeral
Tinsel-thin popular
Songs of a moment
Turned on the tongue
In an undertone
Dying as soon as begun.

In the melancholy
Sliding rain we stood;
You sang –
Your song a requiem
For something mute and vulnerable
Dying as soon as begun...
And I could not speak.

Aunt Sallies

We are the new Aunt Sallies – pelt us
At your pleasure. Here we come – all shapes
And sizes, colours, creeds and cultures.
Cannibal Aunt Sallies – (we admit it, yes)
Attacking one another with the stones
That hurt, the dirt that clings.
Roll up, roll up! Don't pity us –
We're witless; two-dimensional; we're only
Paint and paste;
We mime the programmed phrases
Signifying – what?
Roll up, roll up! And pelt us
With the stones that hurt, the dirt that clings.
Shout, shout with brazen mouths!
The lion goeth about…
But what of him? He's textbook tamed
And impotent. He cannot roar.
You don't respect the lion any more.

Reflections

Journeying the straight rail
I see that other self –
The antiself –
My image reversed
Travelling alongside
Beyond the dim window pane
Effortlessly riding
The countryside,
Sliding through towns and stations,
My constant likeness,
Likeness undetailed
Like some ghoul of past or future
Mocking me
With copycat motions
A voiceless, faded
Imitation of the solid entity
That clogs my endeavours
Dully and daily.

It has no corporeal reality.
I cannot reach it through the glass
Yet it exists
Reflecting my existence
And is forever
The one I make for better for worse
My twin, my doppelganger,
That secret other
Whom I may never know
But who knows me, the self
Who made it what it seems
And cannot change it now.
It keeps me company
And will not let me go,
Significant reminder
Of a Universe divided
And things that might have been.

Old Tadd

October-coloured in the sky blue autumn
Old Tadd, beneath the drops of hawthorn blood,
Wind tanned and stubbled as the corn cut field,
Blinks eyes malt brown in a sloping sun
And squints along the tunnel of his years…

Does not recall
Who spoke this morning, what was said,
What is today, what year. But he can show
A scar, recount the headlong fall
From Deadman's Oak
In Middle Meadow when he was a boy,
And feel the breaking branch and taste his fear.

And calls to mind
The heavy headed orchard in the sun,
Safe in a den of screening grass
His nine years self, white mongrel Gyp
(The sweetness and the savour of the sin!)
Swift tortured toll:
The frenzied swarm that sought its queen
In young Tadd's hideaway.

And he can see
Beneath the mushroom crop of foursquare homes
The broad sweep of the downs where they would ride,
Dickon and he, their horses to a heaving halt
(The wind tossed laughter mocks his memory still.)

And there are things
He knows but cannot tell:
Young strength, old friendships, smooth feel of a gun,
The bristling dogs and still warm fur
Of rabbits, scent of woman's hair...

Scent of many women who were Tadd's;
He does not see
Their vanished faces, hear their silent names.
Their concentrated charms distil
And mingle in a ten years grave.

Essence of womankind
His Jenny has become
The only woman, but he cannot tell
What lilt was in her voice, nor yet
The colour of her eyes.

Now leaning on the gate he gazes through
The slanting sunlight in the brittle air.
Dickon and Jenny are gone, the downs are gone,
The Deadman's Oak was felled long years ago
And grown men do not know the place where it stood;
The autumn sun is not so warm as that warm sun
That warmed a laden orchard fraught with bees,
But he can taste the heady stolen fruit,
And feel a small dog pant between his knees.

The Unexpected

That which we did not expect –
Our own beginning
In the coalescing essences
Of age-spent stars –
Was after all expected
(Colour of eyes, tone of voice,
Our little life upon this little Earth
That by a singular coincidence
Took form and brought forth
Feeling, mind, and something we perceive
As beauty)
And here we are –
Caught in the fluid motion
Of matter and intellect, interconnecting with that
Which we apprehend as Time and Space,
Accepting probabilities as certainties,
Such as the sun will rise (or seem to rise)
And earth exert its pull,
But questioning (sometimes)
The fact of our existence,
As if – in our arrogance – there had to be
A reason.
Yet here we are – are here –
And that which we did not expect –
The beginning of it all – the unexpected –
We need to believe
Was after all
Expected.

Snowfall

For Vivian

First the white petal in shadowed church
Shaken with silence that fulfils
The heart of words and whispered prayer;
Then gentle the snow fell
Gentle as petal's drift,
Sky sinking earthwards meeting upborne flakes.
Gentle the snow lies
Gentle as thoughts that flicker snowflake-like
About white petals in the church.
Give thanks for release of pent-up snow,
Beauty and silence that fulfil
The heart of words unuttered, tears unshed.

If They Would All Just Stop

Perhaps if they all just stopped
And listened really listened
With the lobes of their mind folded back
Like petals exposing the rose
To the potential bee…
But they don't and I can't and the lobes
Of my own inner psyche refold
And the green-hard rose is a bud
Again and unenforceable.

What is it that opens the rose?
I only know that one day
I want to run to the top of a hill
And shout to the world
That the bud was in blossom and the bees at work,
But my tongue couldn't keep such a message
In motion, and the words
Would have plummeted insensible as birds
With my own dismay at my impotency.
They would have offered sympathy
And counselling – why? – why?
If they would all just stop – just stop!
They would hear for themselves,
Then everyone would know
And there would be no more need
Of words.

Teg

I remember Teg on that green seat
At the road's fork (Teg's seat, we always said)
Teg in her overall, hat on her head
(Always the hat) goloshes on her feet.
And there she'd sit – just there where three ways meet –
All chopper-faced and silent as the dead,
Scanning the screaming sky, the valley spread
Below there like a map – eyes dark as peat.

Yes – I remember Tegwen year by year
Always the same – and this broad view's the same;
The same old robin skips along the bough
And gulls still fill the sky. But see just here –
Teg's seat with nettles pushing through the frame,
For Teg is gone, and no one sits there now.

Kites

Sky above the beach is full of shapes
And colour –
No colour without shape.
Kites describing random walks, sky-tugged
Pigtailed geometries, look down
And bob and weave
At me, a stranger straining at the string,
Sand oozing through my toes, and wondering
How this has been,
This holidaying kite-filled sky,
For days, for weeks, perhaps for ever
Before I came,
And here I am
Wind-jostled like the kites,
A soaring spectrum. Or am I
The fist that fastens me
With a wide catenary
To this brown beach frilled with knitted foam?
Should I let go I might fly or else
Plummet to earth, a wounded bunch
Of photons decomposed,
A handful of brittle spars.
But in that fall what ecstasy.
Why then – let go!

Virtual Image

A sample of paper prepared for analysis

Focus down.
The sacrificial sample you've prepared awaits inspection
On the stage-set altar of glass. So focus down.
See the violated entity revealed –
A runic web
Of pale translucent ribbons loosely wound
And sinuous strong strings,
And tiny kernels sparse and comma-shaped,
And jagged bunched bound faggots that assert
A stained brown coarseness here and there
Between the looping strands.

Now focus down
Upon your thought world as you view
These fibres that have been
Routinely shredded, cauterised,
Chafed in the kicking tube,
Iodine-anointed, teased apart,
Now placed for assessment
On the moving stage.

Focus down
As feelings spring sharp-set
Record sensations,
Estimate emotion,
Plunge the eye into sub-sight reckonings
And grasp the likeness
Of your meaning teased apart.
Manipulate the mirror, move the stage. The edges blur.
The rays of light diverge.
You cannot hold the image,
Cannot focus down.

Prediction

You have seen
The torrent of stars on quaking tides at night,
And the flight
Of swifts, the rainbow sheen
Of starlings' wings, snow under sunset –
You have heard
The shrill cadenzas of a solitary lark,
And the dark
Yews weep when night winds stirred, lone unlonely –
You have seen and heard these things…
They were in your eyes together as I burst
Upon your solitude
So that I felt an interloper – crude,
Untimely – when you thrust
Them out of sight and would not meet my look.
I dared not ask – you never told –
What dear reflections occupied you then.
I only knew you could not meet my look, and know
That never will they merge and I behold
Them in your gaze again.

Faces in Firelight

Now the long evening with its old tale told
Settles to silence, and the thoughts repose
In random recollection. Firelight throws
A lure familiar to charm and hold
In enigmatic thrall. Blind shadows mould
The further darknesses, but firelight glows
With nearer lustre in reflected rose
Of eye and lineament and chin's deep fold.

Faces in firelight: faces made serene,
Irradiant with cleansing flames of truth;
Set faces, softened in the molten years,
Recalling mirages that might have been…
Unquenchable the flagrancy of youth –
Beauty untempered now by time and tears.

Nature

The beech stripped of concealing dress
Shines forth in all her nakedness

Back to Back with Earth

When you lay back to back with earth and felt
Its pulse keep time with yours, watching the slow
Perambulations of a ladybird
Along those stalks criss-crossing overhead;
Or waded meadow-deep, intent to find
Shy 'shivery-shakes'* among the seeding grass
And pastel painted blossoms that were yours
For careless gathering in carefree hours;
Or once, when dawdling to the river's edge
Heavy with morning wetness, felt the shock –
The cold moist impact – as a startled frog
Erupted suddenly into your palm;

Did you think then such pleasures – sensuous, small,
Particulate – could end, and would become
As pictures in an antique room? Or think
That in the tug o' war tradition and
Technology would wage in years to come
Your children's children would be losers all?
Those cosy fields that nestled into hedgerows
Busy with burrowing things and bees –
A sky alive with larks – what are they now?
Just faded photographs whose tender tints
Are overlarded with these slabs of bright
And bitter yellows, garish greens,
The charcoal lines of hedges rubbed away,
Larks fallen silent to the mad machines?

Maybe when children's grandchildren are grown
The conflict will have settled, and there'll be
A field of meadow-grass where they can lie
Gazing through leafy stems to a lark-filled sky,
And pressing back to back with Earth will feel
Its strong pulse keeping rhythm with their own.

(*'*Shivery-shakes' was our name for quaking grass. JW*)

Suburban Spring

You'll find Spring in the suburbs too, but there
They like things formal, and won't let it stay.
A country bumpkin in sweet disarray.
Suburban Spring is lopped and pruned, laid bare,
De-daisied, tidied up, made to conform,
As brisk Pygmalions armed with shears and hoes
Bully it into ranks and martial rows
According to the strict suburban norm.
But here and there a slim laburnum lifts
Its yellow dripping fingers to the breeze
That sports amid suburban cherry trees
And piles their fragile petals in pink drifts.
And still a stubborn dandelion head
Glows brazen in a weeded flower bed.

Winter Beech

I know great poets in their time
Have praised the beech tree's pastel prime;
And others equally renowned
Would sing the song of Summer Crowned,
While others still of wide acclaim
Extol the beech in Autumn flame.

And yet for all their metre's flow
I to the Winter woodland go
Where – lissom, shapely –(silver dark
Her fully-fashioned satin bark)
The beech stripped of concealing dress
Shines forth in all her nakedness.

Splendid the beech in Spring and Fall;
But Winter's splendour best of all!

Three Haiku

Snow on the bright hills
Reflecting silver sunlight
Comforts the scarred earth.

Where is the image
Of the bird that flew over
Yesterday's deep pools?

I see in the glass
A stranger's eyes meeting mine –
My image reversed.

Primroses

These came before the passing of the year.
Before November's sullen course was run,
One soulless afternoon of chill no-sun
Discovered them ridiculously here.
Pale aliens, unheralded, unmet –
Impertinent perverseness! – finding room
In crevice of the downward steps to bloom,
Quite out of place. So delicate, and yet
Inviolate. For somehow they survived
The careless crushing of indifferent feet,
The bitter rain and killing frost; the sleet,
The smothering snow. Three winter months they've thrived
And flourished. How these fragile wantons cling
To their prerogative of greeting Spring!

Susie

Your absence is palpable
It has a presence of its own
The sharp insistence of your cries
Set waves in motion beating still
Upon the membrane of time, and I can feel
The purring pressure of your body
Black and white upon my knee.
The air that parted to admit
Your bounding passage
Starts and flickers – it is only
The light wind pouncing at shadows,
Your substance is no longer
A thing to be comprehended physically
But no less real for that.
So suddenly you ceased to be
Imperceptible to sense; not for you
The staring coat, the wearing thin,
The sorrowful journey ending in sleep.
For you it was the sharp division
Of positive and negative, of white and black,
Swift translation to a state of anti-being where
You have existence even yet.
Leaving an emptiness that hurts.
Why mourn the passing of a cat
While humans die?

But all is kindred. All is energy. And there may be
Among the atoms that composed
Your black-and-whiteness some you shared
With heroes dead, or great ones yet unborn.
But in the end we grieve
For that fellow creature-life we loved to love,
And are deprived of loving.
A sudden movement flickers beyond the window.
I know, even as eagerly I look, it is only the wind
Pouncing at shadows.

Peonies

Yes – peonies. Not those that pose
For camera shots against a ground
Of patio shrubs and razored lawns but these
Wild gypsy things unregulatedly encamped
Where grey coarse nettles have been beaten back
And rubbish cleared beside an old dry wall.

They stopped us in our track. There was a crimson shout.
They leapt out suddenly as if they'd been
Meaning all along to spring a surprise –
Great bursting globes of Latin flounces
All shimmering shimmying in the sun.
(Almost indecent the way they carried on.)

Now what were they up to, do you think,
Skulking behind the rubbish we'd just cleared?
Whatever it was they couldn't wait
To be let out at last. And how they celebrate!
When the wind comes down with a swirl and a swoop
Watch them – they're going cock-a-hoop.

Rain

There is a rain that seems not to fall
But cup one's face, as it were,
In a sensuous moist palm,
Seeding the hair with moisture
Almost stealthily.

And there is lunatic rain, tempest-riven,
That rips one's face, as it were,
In a senseless steel claw,
Punishing the body
Almost brutally.

I like the long strong rain
That neither cajoles nor bullies,
But drives itself, as it were,
Single-minded to the ultimate ideal
Purposefully.

Honesty

My cat looks up;
He strokes me with his eyes,
And in their apricot gleam
I see the sun.
I cast no shadow in its blaze
But feel the fire that licks me
Naked to the bone.

My cat looks up;
The creature in his eyes
Contained within himself
Encounters mine.
In mutual exchange he gives
His all – warmth and affection –
These are all he's known.

My cat looks up;
He strips me with his gaze.
Its radiant honesty
Compels me down,
Back to the hairshirt of disguise
Where – shamed – I cannot meet his frankness
With my own.

(*Inspired by Ginger Jake*)

*Walking the Dog**

Now after winter's worn-out welcome
Suddenly earth and atmosphere vibrate with Spring.
And suddenly too in the sympathetic stirrings, surprising very depths
Of both our beings, out we step
The dog and I in order to experience
A mutual throb and thrill.
These celandines exploding in
our path like popping gas jets
with a yellow flame –
these twig-borne ladybirds
like moving drops of blood
Have been stagecrafted overnight
it seems. Or did the fogs of
yesterday obscure their burgeoning?
The terrier treads daintily, sun
warm on slim black flank
her blunt bull nose sniffing
alternately earth and sky
Downhill through beechmast and
fir cones scattered at the roadside.
The terrier sees it first – or senses it rather – the body in
the hedge – a badger's. At first I thought it was a fox
it seemed too brown – too all-of-
a-colour to be a badger.

But there it was – huge and
humped – victim perhaps of
an unsteady driver. And it
lay in the ditch beneath the
hedge where the dead tree,
felled by recent gales, still
remains. Two corpses, while
the spring, alive with twittering
birds and tentative butterflies,
goes on around them. So much
energy in the air this day,
You would think there would
be enough and to spare for
life to live again within
them both. Homeward, we pass
once more the spot, once more
the dog displays taut curiosity
and puzzlement,
then scampers ahead through
celandines that seem to multiply
second by second. Where from
and how? Whence all the energy
that twangs the heart strings
of the universe. Yesterday
there were no celandines,
they had no existence yesterday.

(**The title is mine. Joyce gave it no title. DW*)

Black Swan

We saw
Steeped in the lambent amber
Of summer's final curtain call
A pair of sable swans
Drifting without motion
Making and breaking the mottled mosaics
Under shredded shrubs at a pool's edge.

Red flash of bills in a berried bush
And then we saw
Quick quaking honeycombs
Dip and dub
The dark brocaded plumage as they passed
To shaken sky in the brown deeps.

And now
Preserved for barren days
Obedient to a switch remembrance glows
Upon the screen.
You see
Matured as wine matures
Cellar deep,
The perfect pastoral:
Black Swans In Late September.

But for me
A different imagery – I see
The dark flocks ride – somnolent –
Sun splendoured on the tide
Of that great river half a world away
Where bone bleached beaches bake before the sea.
And 'Koonwarra' is their sounding name.

Clouds

All the blue day I watch the clouds cavort
With jovial gestures, bump and bounce and slide
In ponderous pantomime, attempt to ride
Huge-sailed the waves of air in clumsy sport,
Then losing balance break apart, abort
The effort, turn and recombine, and chide
Companions lagging like slow ships that glide
With negligent decorum into port.

And then? What then? No need to fantasize,
Ascribe to things inanimate a will
And purpose. Now they coalesce and rise
(Amorphous bloated sponges) swelling till
Wind-driven above some dry and distant plain
Their gathered vapours are released as rain.

A Cat

Contemptuous of the fat and droning flies
That beat about your head in ceaseless crowd
I saw you, upright in the hedge, still proud,
Glaring with fierce affronted eyes.

And now a week has passed; unclaimed and cold
You wait here still, with stiff rain-sodden fur,
Grotesquely shrunk, and eyes a filmy blur,
In creeping fungus and foul mould.

Eight silent days since last you pounced or purred,
And have you not been sought or missed at all?
Or maybe still they bang your plate and call
And wonder why you have not heard.

White

White for the unweaned year:
White, milk-white, flooding these folds
Of hills white-breasted under cambric sky;
New lambs new-white – new innocence;
And white in small cool sunlight
Tenderly curls the owl's feather,
Breath-of-morning borne;
And here – see here –
Pearl-perfect in the frost-chalked grass –
Snowdrops shedding holy glow
For Candlemass.

How I Have Yearned for Winter

How I have yearned for winter! When the sorrowful
North-easterly begins its haunting round the house
Moaning at corners, then the memories stir and rise:
To wake, discover ice inside the window frame,
And see one's breath condensing everywhere indoors –
And out-of-doors, in pendant clusters, icicles
Saw-toothed and menacing along the gutter's edge –
To feel again the nipping pain of finger ends
Encased in woollen gloves weighty and stiff with ice –
And cringing toes cramped into sock-stuffed wellingtons –
Numbed nose and stinging eyelids, and that greater pain –
Tender extremities' slow thawing after play!

How I have hungered for those joys and agonies –
To undergo catharsis, know that benison!
They will not come again; Winter and innocence
Have been abolished – there is no rejoicing now.
The old and homeless suffer cold; the affluent
In overheated houses suffer guilt – perhaps.
I suffer from insidious memory which insists
That those were happy mornings when we ran to school
Across a sparkling field where every leaf of grass
Was spiked with ice that cracked and splintered underfoot.
Those dusks came early and we played till dark, sliding
The sloping playgrounds, and then crying with the cold
Went limping home. Now when I hear the sorrowful
North-easterly begin its haunting round the house,
The memories quicken. How I have yearned for Winter!

Zoo

…and now the threadbare camel
Haughty and swaying
Beyond the ivied wall
Behind the patchwork rock-garden
How minutely labelled.

And then maniacal house of parrots
Crudely demented
Beside a scummy lake of squabbling ducks.

Then put away the Agfa,
Pour the Thermos tea and stretch
Upon the sweating grass,
For we have seen…

Inscrutable ape
With supplicating leather palm,
Trunk-thumping pensive elephant
In rhythmic undulation
Switching straw,
The close-eyed monkey, and the padding purring lion
Kittenly playful, warmed by the holiday sun.

And we have seen
The stained-glass silent fish
Floating in dumb dismay,
And creatures gentle-eyed and timid,
Massive beasts, carved crocodile,
And antediluvian enigmatic turtle…

And we have seen
Them look at us,
And we have seen
The sympathetic candour of their gaze
As if to say:
"We see our natures in your pressing selves."

"You are the whole of us
Our force and frailty
Beauty and our baseness.
And here we represent
Detailed analysis of your complexities
That push and stare and point and grin.

And in that after-sunset letting out of breath
When moistened dusk releases sweeter air
We sink upon our straw
Or roost
Or find the comfort of a clammy stone,
And you have gone

And gathered to yourselves
All that we are
And left us, sleeping shells,
Empty of understanding,
Knowing only that we are of you
And knowing too
The pity of it all."

Heartsease

At last the heartsease is over.
The cheeky little face that shone
From blush of May till mid-October
Has vanished from the stones that line the path.
So small the long lawn-grass
Towered above it, the border stones
Seemed wont to crush it, yet it thrived,
So impudently frail, so unaware
What joy it gave, what happy thoughts
Its sweet small face evoked.
But now it's over.
                                    There's a rose
That lingers still above the path,
And one brave daisy keeps the flag
Of summer flying in the border. But
The heartsease is not there; and now I know
That winter's surely come.

Winter Buds

Stark on a spectral twig – here are forlorn
Black skeletons that crumble into dust
At merest touch. Frail corpses, cold, stillborn –
They came too soon; some mean compulsion thrust
Them unresisting to the bitter air.
What hollow hopes of sunshine and delight,
Sweet breeze-tossed summer days and scented fair
Existence made them spring from season's night?
What promise made them yield, frost-fondled, numb,
To blighting Winter's sear and harsh caress?
These foolish eager ones – untimely come
To greet a season that they could not bless!
I brush the petals that were never seen,
And may not know what beauty might have been.

Energies

During the downpour
Mark
How the ripe drops
Swell and recede at their anchorage
Under garden twigs,
Finally
Gather themselves into globes.

Then
Taut in their skins
Some respond
With a bright release
To the pull of earth;
Others wait
The greater energy of the after-sun
To sift their teeming entities
Into air.

(20th February 2009. JW)

Lightning Source UK Ltd.
Milton Keynes UK
UKHW03f0203270418
321709UK00001B/40/P

9 781781 327647